A Tribute to Gandhiji
in verse

Saroj Daulat Ram

Published by:

IOWI
2011

A Tribute to **Gandhiji** *in verse*
by **Saroj Daulat Ram**

Published by   **In Our Words, Inc.**
               inourwords.ca

Design & Layout   **Anindita Modak**

Library and Archives Canada Cataloguing in Publication

Ram, Saroj Daulat
A tribute to Gandhiji - in verse / Saroj Daulat Ram
Poems.

ISBN 978-1-926926-09-4

1. Gandhi, Mahatma, 1869-1948--Poetry. I. Title.

PS8635.A461T75 2011   C811'.6   C2011-906738-2

First Printing, October 2011

All Rights Reserved. Copyright ©Saroj Daulat Ram 2011.
No part of this book may be reproduced in whole or in part, in any form, or stored on any device including digital media, except with the prior written permission of the publisher. Exceptions are granted for brief quotations utilized in critical articles or reviews with due credit given to the author.

PRINTED IN CANADA

Dedication

To my grandchildren
*Anand, Anjali, Sonia,
Monica, Anand, Kashia*

&

Suchin

Mahatma Gandhi

Foreword

It has always been my heart's desire to compile a collection of my poems which honour a man whom I revere as a godly man, a saint in our times, a saviour who delivered his people to freedom.

Being one of those 'people,' an Indian by birth, I share my countrymen's deep gratification that the principles and teachings of our beloved Mahatma is acknowledged and revered around the world. That figure, clothed in simplicity, is a recognizable icon to all people. His message of Satyagraha (non-violent struggle) has underlined many freedom movements in history.

This collection of poems on Gandhiji has been written over many years. This book is my tribute to his memory.

Saroj Daulat Ram
Georgetown, 2011

Gandhi coming out of jail in 1931 with V.A. Sundaram (father-in-law of Saroj Daulat Ram)

Saroj Daulat Ram's husband, Dr. S.V. Anand, (center) and daughters, Anita and Sonia, with Mrs. Indira Gandhi

Gandhiji

A saviour had come
Though we knew it not
A saint had been born
Though we knew it not
He captivated us all
As none had before
O my countrymen! Be strong!

Thus he urged us along
Marching to his victory song

His message was loud and clear
Fortitude! Have no fear!

Bravely we marched along
To the refrain of his freedom song

The promise of freedom was the lure
To end subjugation—they would endure
Detention became a matter of honour
Non-violence was the moral armour
A spinner's wheel was the only weapon
Wear homespun, on yourself rely upon
Knighthoods were spurned
Imperialist honours scorned
India was blessed with this fearless leader
A visionary, a saint, a seer

A nation marched to his victory song
Unarmed, peaceful, strong!

Gandhiji

Godsend—this holy man
Revered by his countrymen
His ascetic ways they understood
Saw him as a man of truth
His garb that of a saint in poverty
In dhoti and chaddor of khadhi
In open chappals he walked miles
Bore pain in silence and dignity
At last a saviour had come
Considered a deity by some
Who spoke the truth
In the language they understood
Said freedom did not come cheap
Many a sacrifice it would need
He filled them with hope
And spread his vision of freedom
They shunned knighthoods
Bestowed on them by foreign rulers
Led by a selfless leader
Bravely they upheld his banner
He was the 'father of the nation'
'Bapu' was his title at Darshan
He was the Mahatma, a great soul
Indians heeded his call
How strange it be, that a man such as he
Be the chosen of the gods
A miracle that graced India's shores.

Gandhiji

O holy one!
O son of India!
I bow to thee
In reverence
We need you now
As we did then
To lead us—the world—again
We need your wisdom
To bring peace
In troubled lands
We need thy strength
To overcome evil
To right the wrongs
As we went astray
We need your truth
To show the light
Peace and harmony
Non-violently

O holy one!
If you did return
To guide
To support
To keep us on the course
You set for us so long ago
If you could return
O holy one!

Gandhiji

In 1922, our hero was put on trial
For inciting his countrymen
To boycott foreign goods
To spin cotton at home
And wear only homespun cloth
Non-violence, non-cooperation
Became inspirational catchwords
He preached the virtues of self-reliance
To build self-confidence
As soldiers of non-violence
They made going to jail a pilgrimage

So the Mahatma was put on trial
As he was led into court
Presided over by Broomfield
Under police escort
The judge bowed to Gandhiji
He pled guilty
It was a privilege and duty, he said
To fight for the freedom of his country
The judge sentenced him to six years
To be served in prison
As our hero was led off
His followers cried
And fell at his feet
They saw triumph in this defeat
They vowed to fight non-violently
Strikes paralysed the economy
The government came to a standstill
As the jails filled up.

Gandhiji

Fortune smiled on this land
A miracle as miracles be
When the gods in heaven sent such as he
To lead India to liberty
This one—the chosen of the gods
In flesh and blood walked
The plains of India
In search of her soul
He found it in lowly huts of the poor
They saw a messiah who led them
On the march of freedom
To reclaim their birthright
His message of truth and non-violence
Restored their self-confidence
Inspired them to crave freedom
Justice for all to reclaim
Mahatma was the name they gave him
The conscience of the world he became
The father of the nation he became
An apostle of peace and non-violence
A reformer, embodiment of righteousness

Now in those lowly huts
His image adorns the walls
They see him as a deity
A saint who knocked at their door
The forgotten were never forgotten
By this man of God.

Gandhi—a life

This chosen of the gods
Walked this earth for seventy-nine years
Mastered his passions
The ones the flesh is heir to
His mission was to espouse
The rights of the underdog
Uplift the downtrodden
He lived in poverty
Took the vow of chastity
So to serve selflessly
Suffering humanity
He respected his adversary
With words—fiery but soft-spoken
He did it as a labour of love
With determination, resolve
A man of peace, of nonviolence
Yet ready to give his life
By fasting unto death
For the freedom of his country
He was a Christian and a Jew
A Muslim and a born Hindu.
His message was his life
And his life had no equal.

Gandhi—on fear

Freedom for India
Was Gandhi's dream
To lift the scourge of fear
From our souls and our hearts
Our moral backbone to strengthen
To stand up to foreign rulers
Of slavery be ashamed
The truth of his words stirred our rage
We no longer wanted to be slaves.
Gandhi raised us from apathy
Pointed to freedom's dawn
Be brave, persevere
Stand up for our rights
Our birthright!
Liberty's bugles were sounded
From every housetop across this vast land
Freedom did come
His dream realized.

Gandhi—the Prophet

A man of truth
Who lived the truth
In thought, word, and deed
His principles were based on
His actions guided by
His search for the truth
For him truth was god
And god was truth
He lived that truth
Till he embodied truth
And truth they say is god.

Gandhi—in England

On travelling abroad
He made three promises to his mother
To abstain from wine and women
And abide by a strict vegetarian diet
At first he tried to be
As an English gentleman of the day
A silk top hat
And silk shirts to wear
He bought a violin
And took lessons
And tried ballroom dancing

Soon the realisation came
To be Indian, was nothing to be ashamed
Gandhi took heed of the inner prompting
Quit playing the English gentleman
Moved to a bedsitter
Cooked his own food
Walked everywhere
As this was good for health
He studied in earnest
At Law at Lincoln's Inn
At the time a choice profession.

Gandhi—leave taking

Her favourite son came to bid farewell
Putlibhai's eyes shone with tears
She took him in her arms
Bade him to stay safe
As he struggled to be strong
His own tears shed
She patted him gently on his cheek
Giving her blessings
'May God be with you, across the seas
Your three vows you must keep'
She was never to know
This would be the last time
She laid eyes on her favourite son
The vows she sought from him
He remained true to
He would obey all his life
He would deny his flesh
The comforts of life
She had begotten
A saint
A future Mahatma
A man who would never be forgotten.

Gandhi—

He made heroes of lowly men and women
With courage they followed his bidding
Lathi-charges they braved
Weaponless
With the force of righteousness
Naked to brutal force
Herded into crowded jails
Many died of wounds on the way
Their crime was a desire for freedom
From exploitation by the imperialists
Equality within the land of their birth
An end to the reign of the foreigner
His message to them
Be proud of your rich heritage
Being Indian is a privilege
Do not ape Western ways
Adopt noble Indian ways
Strive for justice, equality and liberty
Forward march for your country.

Gandhi

He was the chosen of the gods
Emerging on the Indian political horizon
Like a comet who lit our path
He became the prince of hearts
It was he who brought our salvation
Freed us from the fetters of slavery
He reminded us continually
Of common truths
Love one another, he said
Love your opponent as well
Be true to yourself
Love the poor, as yourself
Speak up against unjust laws
Injustice touches us all
Oppose not with violence
But with non-cooperation, nonviolence
By peaceful means, fearlessly
Face the opponent steadfastly
Let the blows rain down on you
From violence you must refrain
Truth and love is a force
Which becomes a formidable force
It can turn enemy into friend
And bring peace to our land.

Gandhi—Divine fire

Even the gods took pity
On the suffering land of India
The ancient land of Buddha
And sent such as he
Who would be their leader
A divine fire burnt in his soul
With which he lit India's soul
The nation was roused by his call
His divine fire touched every heart
He was enshrined in their hearts
His image hung in every home
They bowed before it in Namaste
In prayer of adoration
In prayer of lamentation
It will remain a matter of glory
In the pages of India's history
That once there was a man
Who was a beacon of truth
Along the path of nonviolent struggle
Whom the nation followed
With their heads held high
On their lips a freedom cry
A movement triumphant
India—strong and independent.

Gandhi—wife

Her name was Kasturba
But she was called Ba
She was everybody's Ba
In the ashram at Sabarmati
She looked after everybody
In the big kitchen she prepared
The meals that they shared
They were married at age 13
Stayed married till she died at 75
For Gandhiji and his guests
She prepared all the meals
In his footsteps she walked
His words were her words
His disciplines became hers
His orders became her commands
She had very few demands
Her devotion to the cause was total
During their sixty-two years together
She was his equal
When she was on her deathbed
In prison at Aga Khan Palace, he wept
She refused to take the new wonder drugs
To cure the pneumonia
She is our unsung heroine surely
Who fought for India's liberty
Shoulder to shoulder with Gandhiji

Gandhi—the price of liberty

He was jailed time and again
By successive viceroys of the Raj
Lord Reading underestimated
This man as a spent force
Perceiving the serious rift
Between Hindus and Muslims
A triumph of the policy of divide and rule
The consequence being a
Prolonging of British rule indefinitely
Then Hitler and the Second World War
Changed the world
Gandhi saw a greater threat
Should England lose the war
A victorious England was still
A weaker power, negotiator
Atlee began the process of liberation
Mountbatten the deliberation
Alas not before dividing this ancient land
Into India and Pakistan
The fruits of the policy of divide and rule
Was the partition of India
Independence for two countries
The price that was paid
For liberty.

Gandhi—and Harigens

Harijan was Gandhi's name for them
'Child of God' he called the Dalit
They were Hindus of a lower caste
And were treated as social outcasts.
To live in the ashram at Sabramati
Strict rules must be observed
Of hygiene, fearlessness and austerity
Of abstinence, vegetarianism and charity
When an 'untouchable' couple came
They met the criteria for admission
But the ashramites raised an objection
As too did the ashram's donors
They threatened a boycott
Threatened to withdraw their support
If Untouchables were allowed in.
Gandhi knew he must set the example
That in his eyes all are born equal
Trusting in god he welcomed the couple
But without the patrons support
Money for the upkeep was low
Till one day an anonymous donor
Gave money for a year of support
The ashram was saved
The untouchables stayed.

Untouchability was officially abolished
After Independence.

Gandhi—Indian National Congress

In the 1880s it was formed
The Indian National Congress
By the Englishman Hume
It was created to include India's voice
The right to hear the Indian viewpoint
It became a platform for the elite
Of the educated, the professional, the rich
Who made great speeches
Well-dressed in English attire
They talked to the educated few
Related to but a few
The vast majority knew naught
Of their oratorical promises.
And then came Gandhi in 1914
To shift the paradigm by 1920
Now it was the masses included
In the manifesto of the Congress
Together they knew they must stand
To fight for India's freedom
To become self-sufficient as a nation
To abolish untouchability
To take pride in cottage industry
To make speeches in the mother tongue
To reclaim their birthright
Through Satyagraha –
Nonviolent civil disobedience –
Gandhi's vision was realised
As they rose, a nation, together
FREEDOM was their mantra.

Gandhi—schooling

Schooling was a must in his upbringing
Specially encouraged was learning English
Once an inspector came to test the class
In the standard of English taught
He dictated a series of English words
And Gandhi misspelled some of the words
His teacher prompted him to correct it
By copying from one who had it right
Gandhi ignored the teacher's prompting
For that would be cheating and
By nature he was truthful
And dishonesty was not his way.
Another day his brother and he had sold
Piece of jewellery off his armband of gold
To pay back his older brother's debts
Gandhi, uneasy, confessed to his mother
For he was now troubled by his guilt
Confess to your father, she said
He will beat me you know, if I tell him
He will not slap you if you tell the truth
He will punish you if you hide the truth
Gandhi wrote his confession
On a piece of paper
And took it to the sick bed of his father
Who read it carefully
And was heartened by his child's integrity
Lovingly the father accepted the apology
And his tears washed away
The unease and guilt of his progeny.

Gandhi—Benaras

Banaras Hindu University—
At the opening ceremony of B.H.U.
Were gathered the elite of India
Maharajas, decked in regal finery
Were the major sponsors of the event
Dreams of Malviyaji* had come true
In the building of the B.H.U.
Gandhiji and the Viceroy were present
Extolling the power of learning
Gandhi, dressed in homespun cloth
Reiterated the virtues of vernacular
Higher learning with simple living
Dressing simply
And not in bejewelled finery
The Maharajas who were bedecked
In grand opulence
Felt insulted and humiliated
And rose in indignation
And headed to the door
As the students hailed and cheered.

*refers to Pundit Madan Mohan Malaviya, an Indian politician, educationist and freedom fighter, who founded the Banaras Hindu University (BHU) at Varanasi in 1916.

Gandhi—His Talisman

When doubts assail you
When selfishness overrides good intent
When you are at your wits end
Not knowing the next step
Lost on the road of life
Take a moment to ponder
To recall the face of the poorest
The plight of the weakest
That you may have seen
While passing by mean streets
And ask yourself if the step you are taking
Is for the greatest good of all
Will it their self-respect restore
Will it give them food and shelter
Will it hinder their self-confidence
Will it restore their dignity
So they can take control of their destiny
Never again to go hungry
Will it free them from bondage
To live in freedom from age to age.

Weigh your step by this standard
Then you shall not flounder.

Gandhi—Partition

At midnight of August 15th, 1947
India raised its tri-colour banner
On the steeple of the Red Fort
India was free!
Freedom at last!
But alas – at what cost
The subcontinent had been severed
A nation divided into two
This ancient land of Hindustan
Was separated into India and Pakistan
By the departing former British rulers
The outcome of a policy of divide and rule
Bitter seeds of hatred had been sown
In a land where all had lived side by side
For centuries in communal harmony.
Gandhi was devastated
His beloved India was violated
His life's work for Hindu-Muslim unity
Was in vain with this proclamation
He had fought for India's liberty
But at what price the victory?
His slogan of Hindu-Muslim unity
Echoed faintly across this truncated land
Where blood flowed
And corpses covered the ground.
This was not freedom
Forgotten was his doctrine of non-violence
Now the land was defiled
By this bloody violence

By those who had lived in peace
Side by side for centuries
The worse was in Bengal and the Punjab
That had been divided each into half
Half to India, half to Pakistan
Gandhi began fasting unto death
To stop the violence
Hindus and Muslims came to their senses
And the bloodshed they promised to end
But our hero was a disappointed man
His beloved India was a fractured land
He started to receive death threats
From those who accused him
Who blamed him for the Partition
They blamed him for the bloodshed
This man, who had been sent to jail
By the British time and again
For defying their right to retain
India as a jewel in their crown.
Now this champion of liberty
Was blamed for the costly victory
Like Christ, he turned the other cheek
And visited the dying from street to street
To offer solace and comfort
To tend to their wounds and help heal
He begged for the violence to stop
And to live like brothers as before
The threats to his life continued
Offers of protection he refused
From the Indian government
He vehemently rejected even the mention
Fearlessly, he went on foot everywhere
Into the quarters of the suffering poor

The Hindus accused him
Of a pro-Muslim stand
And for the creation of Pakistan
He was not deterred
As comfort to all he offered
In spite of threats, he still went
And the violence and bloodshed did end
But such were the passions of the times
That resentment soared high

And one day a man, Nathuram Godse
Found his way
To the evening prayers of the day
As Gandhi came out of Birla House
The assassin fired three shots point blank
Into Gandhi's chest, as he bent
In a gesture of greeting
Gandhi uttered the name of God
And fell to the ground soaked in blood
Such was the irony and senseless passion
That a man who always spoke of peace
Was martyred by violence
So ended the life of a freedom fighter
India's hero, the Father of the Nation
So ended the 30th day of January, 1948
A date of infamy in India's history
Only four days before on 26th January
India had proclaimed itself a republic
Gandhi was the chosen of the gods
To the heavens he was recalled
When his mission was completed
When India was at last liberated
He is now revered as freedom's champion
As a martyr, a saint, a beloved icon.

Gandhi—train incident

Some incidents shape our lives
There were three such in Gandhi's
The 'colour bar' ruled in South Africa
When to its shores he first arrived
He felt its bite first hand
As he travelled by train to Pretoria
His ticket was for first class travel
His reserved seat was in comfort
Until a white passenger entered the cabin
Looked in disdain at Gandhi's brown skin
And summoned the ticket collector
To get rid of the 'coloured man'
The guard told Gandhi to move
To third class, where coloureds travelled
Gandhi refused to move
Having paid for First Class travel
He was thrown out on the platform
At Maritzburg at midnight, alone
In the cold dark night of the soul
He debated his options
Should he return to India
Or should he stay and
Bear the scourge of the colour bar
He chose to stay and
Stand tall, join the challenge
Against the racist policies of that land
He stayed twenty years
In a struggle that changed his life
And saw the rise of his abiding philosophy
Of non-violent struggle for freedom.

Gandhi—stagecoach incident

On a stagecoach in South Africa
Gandhi was told to sit near the driver
Being a coloured man
He was not allowed to sit inside
Gandhi refused to sit outside
At the feet of the driver
As his ticket was for a seat inside
The manager started to beat Gandhi
For disobeying his orders
While the others watched
The white passengers took pity on him
And asked him to sit with them inside
For they could not bear to see him beaten
So severely
By the time he reached Pretoria
He was still in shock at the realization
That Indians had no rights
He had found his mission in life
To champion
The cause of the underdog

Gandhi—third defining incident

A third incident that changed
Gandhi's outlook on life
That showed him his mission in life
Was when he was shown the door
By a district collector
Whom in England he had known.

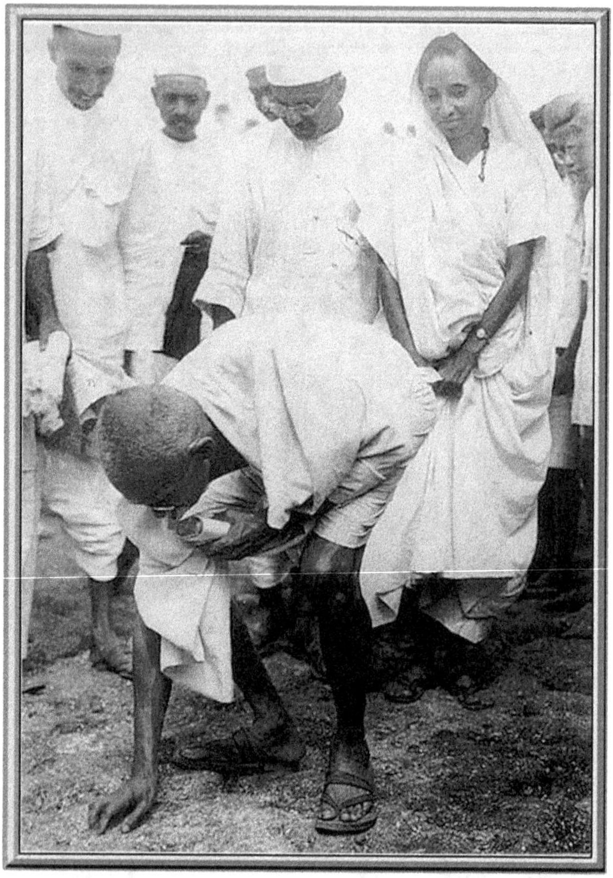

Gandhi—Salt March

It began with the imposition
Of a tax on the sale of salt
By the British rulers
Who cared not that
It was the poor, the oppressed of this land
Who ultimately paid the price
With a heavier burden
For whom a daily meal
Was often a dream unrealised
Gandhiji took the lead
With a proposal that made history
He encouraged his people
To make their own salt
From the waters of the Indian Ocean
That lapped at their shores
He led with two freedom fighters
The march to the sea
His band of brothers grew and grew
Till all of India fired with his passion
For freedom and independence
Joined in the 'Salt March'
Three weeks later
March 12th, 1930, they reached
The shores of Dandy Beach
Gandhiji bent down to pick salt crystals
The symbolic gesture captured
A nation's heart and soul
Spurring the resistance against
The unjust laws of foreign rulers

On this their homeland
Housewives were seen making salt
In their homes
Many were arrested for their defiance
Leaders were beaten by police
The Salt March became a Walk of Freedom
A liberation call against imperialism
The Viceroy Lord Irwin
Misjudged the impact of the March
And the spiralling into a freedom march
The Mahatma had unified a nation
With his powerful weapon
Of non-cooperation
The Salt March showed India
The road to freedom and liberty.

Gandhi—Mahatma

By the year 1920, he was called Mahatma
A super soul, a saint, a rishi
With his vow of poverty
His saintliness and humility
His truth and simplicity
He had won the hearts of rich and poor
They heeded his call
Once at a tour of Bihar
Gandhi's car had a punctured tyre
An old woman of 104 by the roadside
Had waited in rain for long hours
To get a glimpse of this revered man
The great Mahatma Gandhi.
Why do you want to see him, they asked
He is an avatar, an incarnation of god,
She said
I have come for his darshan
To look at his sacred visage
This pilgrimage is for my salvation
To see his holy reflection.
There was mass adoration
Indication of his immense influence
On the soul of India's poor
By 1921, he was venerated
As a deliverer of the oppressed
A man of peace
India obeyed his call
Going to prison became an honour
They would win freedom

Gandhi—Mahatma

On 30th January, 1948
All of India and the world was in shock
When this man of God was slain
While on his way to greet the crowds
On the grounds of Birla House
For eight decades his light had shone forth
To enlighten the land, to encourage reform
An alienation from sinful, alien ways
And a return to simple, native traditions
The crowds came to pay farewell homage
Some wept, some chanted his name
An era had ended, with his martyrdom
The light had been extinguished
By an assassin's hand at freedom's* dawn
As the funeral procession the next day
Wound its march to holy Jumana way
With Gandhi's flower-draped remains
Nehru stood at the honour guard
Weeping openly for the Father of the Land
The funeral pyre was of sandalwood
On a brick platform it was placed
Gandhi's son lit the funeral pyre
The flames rose higher and higher
Gandhiji ki jai was on every lip
As mourners sobbed and wept
The princes and paupers
Shoulder to shoulder they stood
In a spirit of nationhood.

*Freedom's dawn: India had been granted independence from the British a few months earlier in August, 1947

Gandhiji—the man of truth

With his death, Gandhi became
An icon, a symbol of truth and simplicity
For India
For all nations
For all time
He became a legend
In the struggle for freedom
In the overthrow of imperialism
On this land of 500 million
Enslaved by foreign rule
Gandhi saw the injustice
The struggle for independence
He endorsed
Civil disobedience with non-violence
Which paralysed imperial authority
Defined his path of truth
On which he led his nation to freedom.

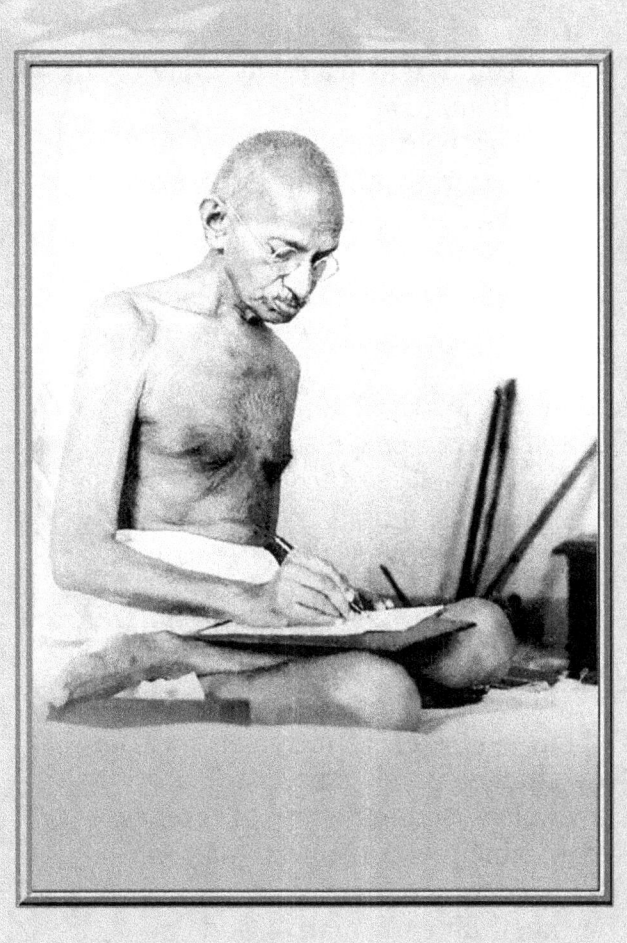

Gandhiji

Even as a child, he was guileless
His cheerful face with a ready smile
Endeared him to all
The truth came naturally to him
His motives were pure, ever transparent
He confessed his faults in humility
Was trusted even by his adversaries
His life was an open book
With instances that showed his true worth
He was a saint in fakir clothing
An unlikely leader of a nation
His weapon was civil disobedience
His message self-reliance
He began a fast unto death
And forced the imperialists to relent
In three weeks they repealed
Their oppressive laws meant to subjugate
Indians, poor and rich alike
He travelled across his homeland
To better know his countrymen's wishes
They chanted his slogans
They welcomed him to humble homes
Recognising their saviour in their midst
His image graced their walls
They knew him as a man of God
Some worshipped him as their lord.

Gandhiji—30th January, 1948

Sixty years ago on this day
An assassin's bullet did slay
India's architect of liberty
He made independence history
As he walked to the prayer ground
Through crowds at Birla house
Nathu Ram Godse, a Brahmin fanatic
Bowed in Namaste and fired at close range
Gandhi fell, his last words 'Hie Ram'
The nation was devastated
A champion of non-violence was slain
The funeral cortege was led by Nehru
Who wept openly as did the crowd
Kings and princes came
As did the homeless to pay homage
Once he had knocked at their door
In his fight for freedom and honour
To reclaim his nation's rights
Through a nonviolent freedom fight
Now on a sandalwood funeral pyre
His son lit the crematory fire
As the crowd chanted Gandhi ki jai
Long live O Martyr Amar Raho, Jai, Jai
On the banks of the holy Jamuna
With the chanting of this holy mantra
They blessed their beloved martyr
As the flames rose higher and higher
His mortal remains were consumed
His memory revered for all eternity.

Gandhiji

He was a saint come to earth
To deliver India in rebirth
To freedom in a new age
To be a free nation on the world stage
He was guided by some higher power
To become his country's freedom fighter.
He paid a heavy price
Made many a sacrifice
To win freedom for his people
Fighting a non-violent struggle
His people responded to his call
And followed his lead steadily
He was revered as a Mahatma
Considered a saint by some
Mothers brought their young to be blessed
By his holy presence in their midst
They erected monuments to him
In the village squares
And renounced English-made attire
In favour of the Gandhi topi
Every farmer proudly wore
The Gandhi dhoti
The chosen language became Hindustani
No longer would they speak in English
Such was Gandhi's hold on the masses
They followed his bidding
Towards his ideals
Of freedom from imperialist rule
Self-rule, self-reliance, independence
He lived to see his dream come true.

Saroj Daulat Ram (second from left, back row) with Rajmohan Gandhi (forefront) grandson of the Mahatma Gandhi

About the Author

Saroj Daulat Ram was born in Jandiala Guru, India. She lived there as a child before moving to East Africa where she lived until relocating to Dublin, Ireland, to begin her medical studies. After receiving her medical degree, she married Dr. S.V. Anand in London, England. She practiced medicine in Nigeria before moving to Nova Scotia, Canada in 1964. While practicing medicine in Nova Scotia, she founded the India-Canada Association. She moved to Ontario in 1985.

Dr. Ram has three daughters and is an accomplished writer, poet and artist.

www.ingramcontent.com/pod-product-compliance
Lightning Source LLC
Chambersburg PA
CBHW071546080526
44588CB00011B/1811